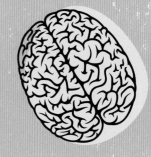

Mind Games

DREAMS and WHAT THEY MEAN

Facts, Trivia, and Quizzes

Elsie Olson

Lerner Publications ◆ Minneapolis

Lerner Publications Company
A division of Lerner Publishing Group, Inc.
241 First Avenue North
Minneapolis, MN 55401 USA

For reading levels and more information, look up this title at www.lernerbooks.com.

Main body text set in Avenir LT Pro
Typeface provided by Linotype

Library of Congress Cataloging-in-Publication Data

Names: Olson, Elsie, 1986- author.
Title: Dreams and what they mean : facts, trivia, and quizzes / Elsie Olson.
Description: Minneapolis : Lerner Publications, 2017. | Series: Mind games | Includes bibliographical references and index.
Identifiers: LCCN 2016051828 (print) | LCCN 2017006755 (ebook) | ISBN 9781512434170 (lb : alk. paper) | ISBN 9781512449396 (eb pdf)
Subjects: LCSH: Dreams—Juvenile literature.
Classification: LCC BF1091 .O47 2017 (print) | LCC BF1091 (ebook) | DDC 154.6/3—dc23

LC record available at https://lccn.loc.gov/2016051828

Manufactured in the United States of America
1-42053-23923-2/20/2017

CONTENTS

Introduction
SWEET DREAMS

It's Tuesday morning, and you're late for school. You slide into your desk as the bell rings. Then you see "Final science exam today!" written on the whiteboard. You panic. You haven't studied at all. Then you notice your teacher is an alien from outer space!

BUZZ BUZZ BUZZ! You sigh in relief to hear your alarm. It was only a dream! But what did it mean?

WHAT ARE DREAMS?

You will spend one-third of your life sleeping. In that time, you will have as many as 100,000 dreams! Dreams are visions and thoughts that happen while you are asleep.

Some people believe dreams can provide important clues to your life. Others think dreams are just **random** thoughts. Either way, scientists agree that dreams are important. And it is fun to try and figure out what they mean!

Chapter 1

DREAMING THROUGH THE PAST

Many cultures have held beliefs about dreams since ancient times. More than 7,000 years ago, people in Mesopotamia wrote clay tablets interpreting dreams. Other cultures shared dreams **orally**.

Aboriginal Australians believed dreamers go on great journeys. Dreamers share these journeys with others to provide them guidance. The Iroquois in North America traditionally believe people can travel to the future and the past in dreams.

VISIONS OF THE GODS

Many ancient people believed gods provided messages about the future through dreams. That meant people took dreams very seriously!

In present times, many religions still include tales about gods communicating with people in dreams. Buddhists believe dreaming can provide training for the **afterlife**.

It's True!

Studies have shown that people dream in both black and white and in color.

DREAMY JOBS

In many cultures, dream interpretation was left to professionals. Ancient Egyptians trained professional dreamers in dream schools to help leaders make important decisions.

Even untrained dreamers could hold great power. In the 1800s, Harriet Tubman said she saw the future in her dreams. After escaping slavery, she used her visions to guide other slaves to freedom.

IS IT SCIENCE?

What made these famous dreamers see the visions they did? Scientists don't know for sure, but dream interpretation has been around for thousands of years.

Could You Be a Pro Dreamer?

Do you have what it takes to be a dreamer and snooze for a job? Take the quiz below. Tally up your points on a separate sheet of paper to find out!

1. Pick an animal.

  A. giraffe *(1 point)*

  B. koala *(2 points)*

2. Pick a bedtime.

  A. 9:00 p.m. *(3 points)*

  B. 11:00 p.m. *(2 point)*

  C. I just go to sleep when I'm tired. *(1 point)*

3. What time is your alarm clock set for?

  A. 9:30 a.m. *(2 points)*

  B. 7:00 a.m. *(3 points)*

  C. What alarm clock? *(1 point)*

4. Can you remember a dream from last night?

  A. Yes, totally! *(3 points)*

  B. I can a little, kind of. *(2 points)*

  C. What dream? *(1 point and skip to question 6)*

5. How many details can you remember from your dream? (Think of details related to taste, sight, sound, smell, and touch.)

  A. 1–3 *(1 point)*

  B. 4–5 *(2 points)*

  C. 6 or more *(3 points)*

6. Can you remember any dreams from last week?

  A. Sure, which one? *(3 points)*

  B. I think so. One, maybe? *(2 points)*

  C. Are you kidding? I can't remember what I ate for lunch yesterday. *(1 point)*

7. Have you ever had a dream that seemed to tell the future?

  A. No way. *(1 point)*

  B. Sort of, but I'm not sure. *(2 points)*

  C. Yes! It was kind of spooky. *(3 points)*

6–10 Points: Dream On! You have your work cut out for you if you want to be a pro dreamer. Go to bed at a regular time and get enough sleep to help remember your dreams.

11–15 Points: Pro . . . with Practice. You're almost there, but you have room to improve. Try keeping a dream journal. Write down your dreams as soon as you wake up.

16–20 Points: Super Skilled Snoozer. You're ready for the big leagues! You have **vivid** dreams, and you remember them. Make sure to write your dreams down. This will help you notice any patterns.

Chapter 2

THE SCIENCE OF SLEEP

Have you ever heard your dog bark in her sleep? If so, she might have been dreaming about chasing a squirrel. Scientists know that many animals other than humans dream. This includes dogs, cats, and mice.

SLEEP OR DIE!

Scientists also know that all mammals and birds need some kind of sleep. However, they don't know exactly why. Scientists do know that if people and most animals do not sleep, they will eventually die!

BUSY BRAINS

Scientists learn about sleep and dreams in humans using sleep studies. They observe people as they sleep. They measure the sleeper's heart rate, body temperature, eye movements, and brain waves. Thanks to these studies, we know that your brain is very active while you're sleeping.

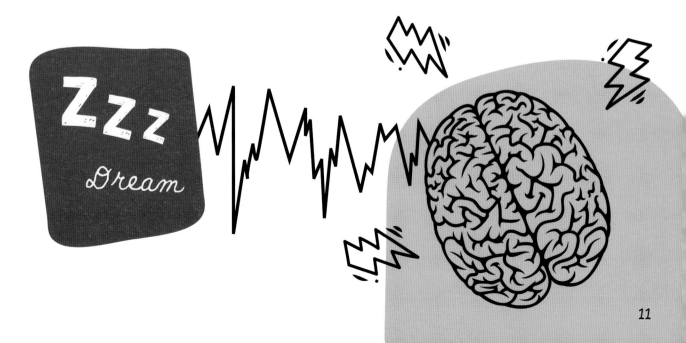

Sleep Cycles

Sleep studies have shown that people sleep in cycles. Each cycle has four stages. Most dreams happen near the end of the cycle.

Stage 1

Light sleep lasting five to ten minutes. Your brain is active during this time, and you will be easy to wake.

Stage 2

Deeper sleep with less brain activity. Your body temperature drops. Your heart rate slows. This stage lasts about twenty minutes.

Stage 3

Very deep sleep. You have no muscle movement. It will also be very hard to wake you up. This stage lasts about thirty minutes.

Stage 4 (REM)

Rapid eye movement (REM) sleep. Your eyes move very quickly during this stage. It lasts between ten minutes and an hour.

The brain is very active during REM sleep. Because of this, scientists believe most dreams occur during this stage.

If you are woken during REM, you will be more likely to remember your dreams. If you keep sleeping, you will cycle back into stages 2, 3, and 4.

It's True!

It takes the average person about seven minutes to fall asleep.

Chapter 3
WHY DO WE DREAM?

Many people have claimed to use dreams in helpful ways. Others feel dreams are random. So why do we dream? **Psychologists** have been seeking the answer to this question for a long time.

FREUD SAYS...

Sigmund Freud was an Austrian psychologist. He developed a dream theory in the late 1800s. Freud believed the mind was like an iceberg. The top of the iceberg is the small part seen above water. Freud compared this to the thoughts we are aware of.

The bottom of the iceberg is much larger. It is hidden from view, underwater. Freud compared this part to thoughts we don't realize we are having. Freud believed dreams reflect these thoughts.

JUNG SAYS...

Carl Jung was a Swiss psychologist. He developed a dream theory in the early 1900s. Jung believed dreams could help people better understand themselves.

Jung felt every image in a dream represented a part of the dreamer. By thinking about what is happening in your everyday life, you can figure out what these images mean.

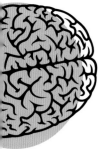

INTERPRET IT YOURSELF!

Anyone can try out dream interpretation. Many books and websites feature dream guides and dictionaries. Try using them to decide what your dreams might mean!

What Do Dreams Mean?

The most important part of your dreams is what they mean to you. Try your hand at dream interpretation with this quiz! Write your answers on a separate sheet of paper. Then compare your results to the answer key below.

1. You dream that you visit the beach with pop star Joe Jonas. What does this mean?

- A. You wish you were famous.
- B. You like Joe Jonas.
- C. You feel like you need to make new friends.

2. You dream you are eating an anchovy pizza, even though anchovies gross you out. What does this mean?

- A. You wish your life was more exciting.
- B. You went to bed hungry.
- C. You feel like you don't try enough new things.

3. You dream that you fall off your bike. What does this mean?

- A. You wish you were a better athlete.
- B. You don't know how to ride a bike.
- C. Something in your life is going in the wrong direction.

4. You dream about an animal. Is it:

- A. a purple unicorn wearing a backpack
- B. your pet cat snuggling in your lap
- C. a grizzly bear chasing you through the forest

5. You dream that your babysitter is a werewolf. What does this mean?

- A. You wish your parents trusted you to be home alone.
- B. You watched a monster movie before bed.
- C. You need more **confidence** in yourself.

Mostly Cs:
Like Jung, you think the images in your dreams represent parts of your personality.

ANSWERS:

Mostly As:
Like Freud, you think dreams can tell you about your hidden wants.

Mostly Bs:
You take your dreams literally. For you, a pizza is just a pizza, and that's a good dream!

Chapter 4

DREAM SYMBOLS

You will have thousands of dreams in your lifetime. You may notice that you have certain dreams over and over again. In fact, some common dreams are shared by people all over the world! What do these dreams mean?

NAKED?!

Did you dream that you are naked in public? This is a very common dream. To understand it, try to remember how you felt during the dream. Were you embarrassed? This may mean you are feeling **insecure**. Did you feel happy? This may mean you are confident.

ON THE RUN!

If you dream of being chased, it could mean you're avoiding something in your life. The next time you have this dream, try to remember who or what was chasing you. This can help you understand who or what you are avoiding.

It's True!

Have you ever had a **nightmare**? Scientists believe these scary dreams are caused by many different things. These can include **stress**, medication, too little sleep, and even late-night snacks!

FALLING

A falling dream can mean that you feel something in your life is headed in the wrong direction. It suggests it's time to make a change in your life.

FLYING

A dream where you are flying can be really fun. It also suggests that you feel confident. Way to go!

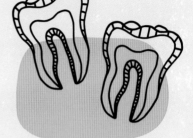

TEETH FALLING OUT

If you've dreamed that your teeth fell out, you might think it's time to see a dentist. But it can also mean you've said things you shouldn't have. This dream could be a sign it's time to **apologize**.

What Does that Dream Mean?

What do you dream about? Follow the question path below to find out what images in your dreams mean.

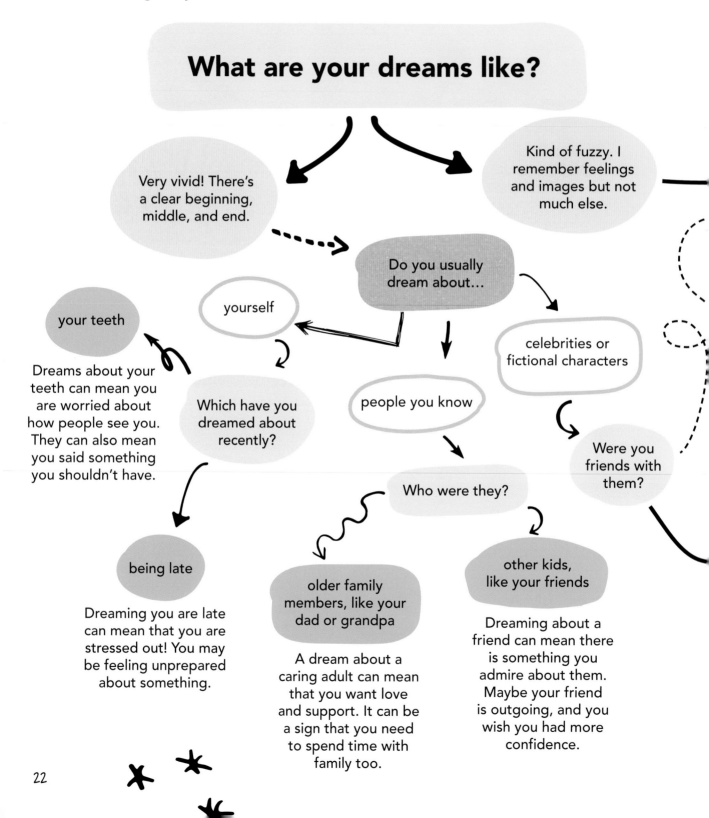

What are your dreams like?

Very vivid! There's a clear beginning, middle, and end.

Kind of fuzzy. I remember feelings and images but not much else.

Do you usually dream about...

yourself

your teeth

Dreams about your teeth can mean you are worried about how people see you. They can also mean you said something you shouldn't have.

Which have you dreamed about recently?

people you know

celebrities or fictional characters

Were you friends with them?

Who were they?

being late

Dreaming you are late can mean that you are stressed out! You may be feeling unprepared about something.

older family members, like your dad or grandpa

A dream about a caring adult can mean that you want love and support. It can be a sign that you need to spend time with family too.

other kids, like your friends

Dreaming about a friend can mean there is something you admire about them. Maybe your friend is outgoing, and you wish you had more confidence.

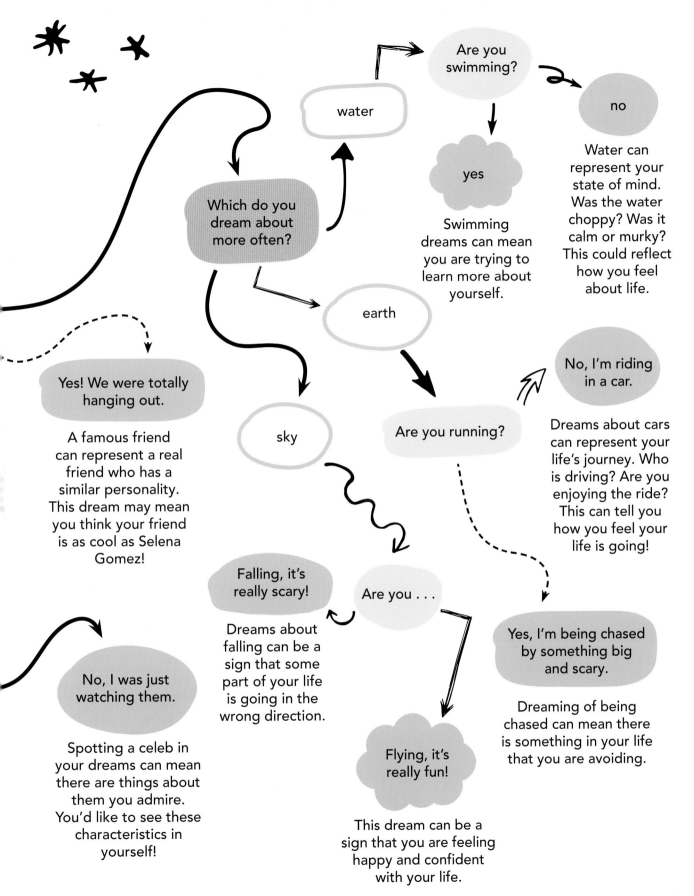

Are you swimming?

water

no

Water can represent your state of mind. Was the water choppy? Was it calm or murky? This could reflect how you feel about life.

yes

Swimming dreams can mean you are trying to learn more about yourself.

Which do you dream about more often?

earth

No, I'm riding in a car.

Yes! We were totally hanging out.

A famous friend can represent a real friend who has a similar personality. This dream may mean you think your friend is as cool as Selena Gomez!

sky

Are you running?

Dreams about cars can represent your life's journey. Who is driving? Are you enjoying the ride? This can tell you how you feel your life is going!

Falling, it's really scary!

Are you . . .

No, I was just watching them.

Dreams about falling can be a sign that some part of your life is going in the wrong direction.

Yes, I'm being chased by something big and scary.

Spotting a celeb in your dreams can mean there are things about them you admire. You'd like to see these characteristics in yourself!

Flying, it's really fun!

Dreaming of being chased can mean there is something in your life that you are avoiding.

This dream can be a sign that you are feeling happy and confident with your life.

Chapter 5

DREAMING THE FUTURE

Have you ever had a dream come true? Many people have claimed to see the future in their dreams. Some have said they had warning dreams before tragedies.

WARNING OR COINCIDENCE?

Most scientists think dreaming about future events is just **coincidence**. With so many people dreaming every night, some dreams are bound to match up with real events. And people are more likely to share their dreams when they seem to come true.

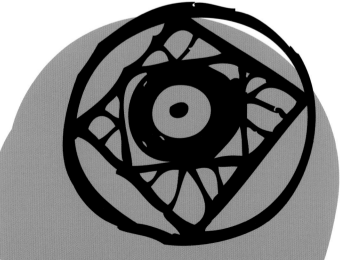

It's True!

Lucid dreaming is when dreamers realize that they are dreaming. They are then able to control events in the dream. Most people have at least one lucid dream in their lifetime.

Chapter 6
DREAM ON!

Can dreams **predict** the future? Can they tell you about your inner wants? Or are they just random? You can decide for yourself! Whether dream interpretation is fact or fiction, it can be a new way to think about your life. You can determine what your dreams mean to you.

interpret

DREAM, DISCUSS, AND DISCOVER

Dreams can be a fun way to learn about yourself. You can also use dreams to learn more about others. Try sharing your dreams with your family and friends. Then ask them to share their dreams with you. You might find new meanings you hadn't thought of on your own. Have fun exploring your dreams, and soon you will be an expert on you!

Make Your Own Dream Journal!

The first step to interpreting your dreams is remembering them. A dream journal is a great way to record your dreams!

Materials:

- notebook
- supplies for decorating, such as glue, markers, feathers, and glitter
- pencil
- headlamp or reading light

Step 1: Start by decorating your journal however you like. Be creative!

Step 2: On each page, set up a **template**. Your template should have the following categories:

Date: *(when you had the dream)*
Dream title: *(make it fun)*
Who was in the dream: *(all the people or animals you can remember)*
Where it took place: *(describe the setting)*
What happened: *(describe the events)*
Details: *(list as many details as you can remember, thinking about your five senses of taste, touch, sound, sight, and smell)*
Feelings: *(describe how you felt during and after the dream)*

Step 3: Try to record your dreams as soon as you wake up. Don't worry if you need to leave some categories blank. Just write down what you can remember.

Step 4: Keep the journal near your bed. Store a pencil and a small light with it. This way you'll be ready to record as soon as you wake up!

Step 5: Review your dream journal once a month. Look for patterns. What could these patterns tell you about yourself?

GLOSSARY

aboriginal: being the first or earliest known people in a region

afterlife: an existence after death

apologize: to say you are sorry about something

coincidence: an occurrence of events that happen by accident but seem to have some sort of connection

confidence: a strong belief in your own abilities

insecure: anxious or uncertain about yourself and your abilities

nightmare: a scary or unpleasant dream

orally: using speech

predict: to say what will happen in the future

psychologists: people who study human emotions, behaviors, and minds

random: without order or purpose

stress: mental or emotional strain or pressure

template: a document or pattern used to create similar documents

vivid: sharp and clear

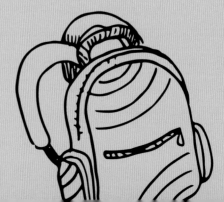

FURTHER INFORMATION

Brynie, Faith Hickman. *101 Questions about Sleep and Dreams That Kept You Awake Nights—Until Now*. Minneapolis, MN: Twenty-First Century Books, 2006.

This book answers questions from students around the United States to teach you amazing facts about sleep and dreams.

Dreams: Why Do We Dream?

http://pbskids.org/itsmylife/emotions/dreams/article2.html

Find out why you dream and even what your dreams could be saying about you!

Most Animals Sleep, But Do Insects?

http://discoverykids.com/videos/most-animals-sleep-but-do-insects

Do insects sleep? Find out by watching this fun video!

Saldarini, Suzanne. *About Dreams*. Fresh Meadows, NY: ORI Academic Press, 2013.

Learn all about dreams and nightmares and what they could tell you about your feelings.

Sleep for Kids

http://www.sleepforkids.org/html/dreams.html

Learn all about sleep and dreams by visiting this fun website from the Sleep Foundation.

INDEX

Photo Acknowledgments

The images in this book are used with the permission of: Design elements and doodles © advent/Shutterstock.com, barkarola/Shutterstock.com, Dina Asileva/Shutterstock.com, Fears/Shutterstock.com, IgorKrapar/Shutterstock.com, ipayo/Shutterstock.com, josep perianes jorba/Shutterstock.com, lineartestpilot/Shutterstock.com, mhatzapa/Shutterstock.com, Mighty Media, Inc., Nikolaeva/Shutterstock.com, Sashatigar/Shutterstock.com, Thumbelina/Shutterstock.com, Vector Tradition/Shutterstock.com, and whitemomo/Shutterstock.com; © hanapon1002/Shutterstock.com, p. 1; © francisblack/iStockphoto.com, p. 3; © imtmphoto/iStockphoto.com, p. 4 (top); © Photographee.eu/Shutterstock.com, p. 4 (middle); © kwanchai.c/Shutterstock.com, p. 4 (bottom); © FatCamera/iStockphoto.com, p. 5 (top); © PeopleImages/iStockphoto.com, pp. 5 (bottom), 8; © paulaphoto/Shutterstock.com, p. 6; © In Green/Shutterstock.com, p. 7; © Vasek Rak/Shutterstock.com, p. 10; © STEEX/iStockphoto.com, p. 14; © Max Halberstadt/Wikimedia Commons, p. 15; © Public Domain/Wikimedia Commons, p. 16; © Syda Productions/Shutterstock.com, p. 20; © Ales-A/iStockphoto.com, p. 21 (top); © asiseeit/iStockphoto.com, p. 21 (bottom); © Shvets Anna/Shutterstock.com, p. 25 (top); © skynesher/iStockphoto.com, p. 25 (bottom); © pixdeluxe/iStockphoto.com, p. 26; © GagliardiImages/Shutterstock.com, p. 27; © Weekend Images Inc./iStockphoto.com, p. 29; © martin-dm/iStockphoto.com, p. 31.

Front cover: © francisblack/iStockphoto.com (top, left); © hanapon1002/Shutterstock.com (top, right); © Purestock/Thinkstockphotos.com (bottom, right).

Back cover: © STEEX/iStockphoto.com (top); © paulaphoto/Shutterstock.com (middle); © Vasek Rak/Shutterstock.com (bottom).